SPORTS INJURIES:
HOW TO PREVENT, DIAGNOSE, & TREAT

EXTREME SPORTS

Sports Injuries:
How to Prevent, Diagnose, & Treat

- Baseball
- Basketball
- Cheerleading
- Equestrian
- Extreme Sports
- Field
- Field Hockey
- Football
- Gymnastics
- Hockey
- Ice Skating
- Lacrosse
- Soccer
- Track
- Volleyball
- Weight Training
- Wrestling

**SPORTS INJURIES:
HOW TO PREVENT, DIAGNOSE, & TREAT**

EXTREME SPORTS

CHRIS McNAB

MASON CREST PUBLISHERS
www.masoncrest.com

Mason Crest Publishers Inc.
370 Reed Road
Broomall, PA 19008
(866) MCP-BOOK (toll free)
www.masoncrest.com

First printing

1 2 3 4 5 6 7 8 9 10

Library of Congress Cataloging-in-Publication Data on file
at the Library of Congress

ISBN 1-59084-630-3

Series ISBN 1-59084-625-7

Editorial and design by
Amber Books Ltd.
Bradley's Close
74–77 White Lion Street
London N1 9PF
www.amberbooks.co.uk

Project Editor: Michael Spilling
Design: Graham Curd
Picture Research: Natasha Jones

Printed and bound in the Hashemite Kingdom of Jordan

CONTENTS

Foreword

Sports Injuries: How to Prevent, Diagnose, and Treat is a seventeen-volume series written for young people who are interested in learning about various sports and how to participate in them safely. Each volume examines the history of the sport and the rules of play; it also acts as a guide for prevention and treatment of injuries, and includes instruction on stretching, warming up, and strength training, all of which can help players avoid the most common musculoskeletal injuries. *Sports Injuries* offers ways for readers to improve their performance and gain more enjoyment from playing sports, and young athletes will find these volumes informative and helpful in their pursuit of excellence.

Sports medicine professionals assigned to a sport that they are not familiar with can also benefit from this series. For example, a football athletic trainer may need to provide medical care for a local gymnastics meet. Although the emergency medical principles and action plan would remain the same, the athletic trainer could provide better care for the gymnasts after reading a simple overview of the principles of gymnastics in *Sports Injuries*.

Although these books offer an overview, they are not intended to be comprehensive in the recognition and management of sports injuries. The text helps the reader appreciate and gain awareness of the common injuries possible during participation in sports. Reference material and directed readings are provided for those who want to delve further into the subject.

Written in a direct and easily accessible style, *Sports Injuries* is an enjoyable series that will help young people learn about sports and sports medicine.

Susan Saliba, Ph.D., National Athletic Trainers' Association Education Council

A skydiver plummets towards earth. During the fall, his body will achieve speeds of 160 miles per hour (257 km/h).

Extreme Sports as a Pastime

The term "extreme sports" is relatively new and refers to activities that contain a higher degree of danger than conventional sports. These range from surfing to parachuting, and are becoming increasingly popular with young athletes.

Some extreme sports are very unusual. One current sport is "extreme ironing," which involves competitors battling to see who can iron in the most demanding natural environment. Fearless individuals climb sheer mountain faces carrying ironing boards, battery-powered irons, and a load of crumpled clothing. Once at the summit, they set up the ironing board and do the ironing.

In this book, by contrast, we will look at the extreme sports that are practiced by thousands of individuals worldwide. Although we cannot look specifically at every extreme sport available, some of the most popular follow.

ROCK CLIMBING

Climbers generally make the headlines when they scale huge snow-capped mountains, such as Everest or K2. Such expeditions often cost hundreds of thousands of dollars and require advanced technical expertise. Rock climbing is the more popular and less expensive alternative.

A climber moves up the face of Mount Everest. Everest is the world's highest mountain, rising to 29,029 feet (8,884 m), and was first climbed in 1953 by Sir Edmund Hillary and Tenzing Norgay.

A sport that is open to all ages and abilities, rock climbing has several different styles, but is most popularly known as "free climbing." In free climbing, the climber makes his own way up the rock face without artificial aids—only safety equipment is used. Climbing is usually done in pairs. One person will ascend the rock face, installing **pitons** and **carabiners** into the rock at regular intervals and fitting a safety rope through them. At an agreed point, the climber will halt and make himself secure, then his companion will climb up from below, using the established rope as a safety device in the event of fall. This climber will also collect the pitons and clips as he goes. Once he has reached the first climber, the two repeat the process again, moving to the top of the cliff. The technique is known as **belaying**.

Descent is by either a reverse of this technique or **rappelling**. During rappelling descents, a climber basically walks down the cliff face, attached to a long double rope

Rock climbers must be able to look at a rock face and plan a route to the summit using the best available handholds and footholds.

that is securely fastened to a belaying point. He controls the speed of his descent using a piece of equipment known as a **descender**, which is attached to the rope.

Rock climbing takes place on natural rock faces and also on artificial climbing walls that are approximately eighty-two feet (twenty-five meters) in height. Artificial indoor walls are used in the growing sport of competition climbing, in which climbers compete against one another in speed of ascent and descent.

In terms of sports injuries, the most serious dangers for rock climbers come from falls. However, strains, sprains, and injuries to the hard-worked hands, legs, and back are more common problems.

PARACHUTING

The first parachute jump was made from a hot-air balloon by the Frenchman André Jacques Garnerin in 1797, but it was not until the advent of aircraft in the early twentieth century that parachuting became widespread. In the 1930s, Russia, Italy, and Germany developed reliable parachute technology and techniques, mainly for use in the military. Military parachuting was the principal application until after World War II, when people became aware of the sporting potential. In 1951, the first world parachuting championship was held.

The object of this first championship was for parachutists to demonstrate accurate landings on a circular area, after a jump from about 3,280 feet (1,000 m)—the winner being the man or woman who landed closest to the center point of the circle. Since then, accuracy-landing competitions have become regular events in the parachuting calendar, and other types of events have also been added.

There are **free-fall** events in which parachutists have to either perform a prearranged set of aerial techniques or demonstrate their own techniques during the drop. They are judged on artistic merit and technical skill.

Skysurfing is a true extreme sport. For safety, the board is fitted with an emergency release mechanism to be used if the parachutist goes into an uncontrollable spin.

There are also team events, such as formation skydiving and canopy formation. In the former, up to sixteen parachutists make choreographed patterns or formations in the sky, having jumped from between 9,840 feet (3,000 m) and 12,470 feet (3,800 m). By contrast, canopy formation teams of four or eight parachutists actually hold hands with one another or touch another's parachute with their feet. During the descent, they create different formations. In some events, the members of the team must form a stack and rotate each person's position in the stack before touching the ground.

Two final—and spectacular—categories of parachuting are **sky surfing** and **paragliding**. The sky surfer makes a free-fall jump from an aircraft with what is, in effect, a surfboard attached to her feet. As she falls, she uses the board to surf through the air and perform acrobatics before opening the parachute. The paraglider uses a special parachute shaped like an aircraft wing. He launches himself from a high piece of ground or from a winch, and then flies the parachute in an intricate display of aerobatics. In competitions, the paraglider must steer his chute around a prearranged aerial course. A camera set in a fixed position photographs the paraglider at key points to make sure that the various stages of the course have been passed correctly.

SURFING

Surfing is not often thought of as an extreme sport, but the dangers are very real. Surfers must endure freezing seas, lethal tidal currents, mountainous waves, razor-sharp rocks just beneath the surface, and the ever-present threat of drowning.

Surfing, whether as a ritual or as a way of fishing, stretches back for centuries—Captain Cook gives an account of surfers seen during his voyage to Hawaii in 1798. In the first decade of the twentieth century, surfing saw an upsurge along the shorelines of Hawaii once more as men such as Duke Kahanamoku reignited interest in the sport. By 1920, Hawaii had its own surf club, and the sport was spreading across the world as far as Australia. The real explosion in surfing came in the 1960s. Heavy wooden boards weighing up to 154 pounds (70 kg) were replaced by light synthetic boards made of materials such as polystyrene and fiberglass. Some of these modern boards weigh less than 2 pounds 3 ounces (1 kg)!

With inexpensive and manageable boards now available, surfing took off as an international sport. In the United States, the International Surfing Committee—now known as the International Surfing Association (ISA)—was formed at Palm Beach, Florida, in 1960. World championships began shortly afterward. The biggest competition is currently the ISA's World Surfing Games.

There are three basic categories of surfboard. The Longboard is used by beginners because of its stability in the water, and is a minimum of 9 feet (2.75 m) long. The Shortboard, at 5 feet 11 inches (1.8 m) long, is far more maneuverable but much less stable, and is the choice of professionals. Finally, in a category all its own, is the Bodyboard. Normal surfing usually requires the surfer to lie flat on the board to swim out to sea, then stand up to surf back into the beach. The Bodyboarder remains lying down at all times, steering the board through the waves by shifting her body weight and angling the front of the board with her hands.

SKIING

Skiing was an ancient method of travel at least 2,500 years before the Christian era, and appears to have originated in the frozen climates at the extreme north of Europe. Today, snow mobiles and other off-road vehicles have almost entirely replaced skis for travel, but skiing remains as the world's most popular winter sport. During the twentieth century, skiing developed into a varied range of

Surfing is one of the world's most popular extreme sports. The surfer here has just performed a 'cutback' maneuver, whipping up to the crest of the wave, then turning back sharply.

sporting events, with international competitions beginning in 1931 after the formation of the International Ski Federation seven years earlier.

Skiing has several branches:

- Downhill skiing is a descent down a mountainside (usually following a set course), and the aim is speed.
- There are several categories of slalom, in which the skier weaves in and out of posts set into the snow at regular intervals.
- In freestyle skiing, skiers perform complex turns and jumps, often using specially constructed snow ramps to get maximum lift-off for aerial techniques.

- Speed skiing is a true extreme sport: the skiers descend almost vertical slopes and compete to see who can attain the fastest velocity. Speeds in excess of 124 miles per hour (200 km./h.) are common.

- Ski jumping is a spectacular sport in which the skier jumps from the end of a large, steep takeoff ramp and attempts to make as much distance as possible. Ski jumping demands tremendous skill to remain stable in flight and to land safely.

- Cross-country skiing is about stamina more than speed. The competitors ski across fairly flat courses up to 31 miles (50 km) in length. Depending on the style of

Ski jumping is not for the fainthearted. Exceptional balance is required to stay in the proper flight position during the three or four seconds a jumper is in the air.

event, they use a mixture of sliding, pushing, poling, and skating actions to propel themselves. They are athletes of the highest order, and need the stamina of marathon runners to maintain the speeds needed for victory.

Rock climbing, parachuting, surfing, and skiing are only four of a wide range of extreme sports. Others include diving, bungee jumping, and some forms of skateboarding and rollerblading. All involve a high degree of danger, and so must be practiced with caution, intelligence, and a total respect for safety.

SNOWBOARDING

Snowboarding emerged in the 1960s and has gone on to become one of the most popular winter sports among young people. It is essentially a form of skateboarding across snow, using a snowboard. The direction of the snowboard is controlled by the snowboarder altering his weight and balance. There are two types of snowboard. A Freestyle board is 4 feet 4 inches to 5 feet 2 inches (1.34–1.58 m) long and 9 $^3/_8$ inches (24 cm) wide and is used for more acrobatic snowboarding. The Alpine board is longer, at 4 feet 9 inches to 5 feet 9 inches (1.45–1.75 m), and narrower, at 7–7$^3/_4$ inches (18–20 cm), and is capable of achieving higher speeds than the Freestyle board. Competitive snowboarding features a variety of events:

- Freestyle competitions focus on demonstrations of acrobatic techniques.
- Alpine snowboarding is a speed event on different downhill courses.
- Freeride snowboarding takes place on natural slopes—the snowboarder is awarded points for his or her negotiation of natural obstacles.

Snowboarding had its first world championship in 1992 and entered the Olympic Games in 1998. Here a snowboarder performs an aerial maneuver.

Mental Preparation to Prevent Injury

Many accidents in extreme sports occur because of a lack of planning. Extreme sports such as parachuting and mountain climbing require meticulous preparation. Lapses in concentration during extreme sports can have fatal consequences.

Train yourself to examine every possible risk you might face, however unlikely, and think of ways to remove those risks, well in advance of setting out.

For example, before embarking on a rock-climbing expedition, there is a range of factors to consider, including:

- The weather conditions forecast on the day or days of the activity.
- The remoteness of the location.
- The type of equipment you will need for the climb. Do you need to purchase anything? Has your existing equipment been well-maintained?
- What means do you have of communicating with rescue services should you need them?
- The characteristics of the rock face, including its height, the type of rock, and whether the climb includes overhangs.
- The type of survival equipment needed. Who will be responsible for the individual items?

Mountain bikers need exceptional levels of strength in the legs. They must also be able to concentrate hard during fast downhill rides to avoid potentially lethal obstacles.

This list is only a fraction of what you might have to assess for your expedition. Write down every item of equipment and every preparation you must make on a checklist. Put a check box by the side of each item, and check off that item only when it is packed or completed. In any extreme sport, the first way to prepare wisely is to take expert advice. Never undertake an extreme sport without the guidance of an experienced instructor.

The best mental planning you can do to reduce your likelihood of injury is to mentally rehearse how you would cope with any disasters. Scientific research has shown that people cope better with sudden traumatic demands if they have mentally prepared in advance to face them.

Do this by picturing the potential problems which might face you, but see yourself coping with them confidently and boldly. For example, imagine that you

Spend time doing research to find out as much as possible about your extreme sport. Do not, however, slavishly follow book advice without checking it first with your instructor.

are out surfing when a powerful **rip tide** starts to drag you out to sea. Picture the scene as clearly as possible: the coldness of the sea on your body; the noise of seabirds; the salty taste of the seawater on your lips; the pull of the rip tide against your body. The more vividly you "see" and "feel" the scene in your mind's eye, the better your response will be in real life because your mind will tell you that you have coped with the situation before.

Instead of panicking, picture yourself responding with calm confidence to the situation, using the correct technique, which is to swim diagonally across the beachfront until you reach a piece of headland farther along. Swimming straight in toward the beach will not help because the current will hold you back until you are exhausted.

By going through the problem and the solution to rip tides in your mind, you are far more likely to stay calm and choose the correct techniques to save your life if you should actually experience a rip tide. This principle applies to all sports. In real-life crises, however, a problem for many people is how to handle fear.

HANDLING FEAR

In extreme sports, fear is a major threat to your safety. Of course, fear has a useful function. It can warn you that something is too dangerous to try. However, it can also paralyze and confuse you at times when you need to think clearly in order to protect yourself. If you do extreme sports, this paralysis can be lethal. The first point to realize is that fear is your friend, not your enemy. It prepares the body for action, making it stronger and faster. The key is to take control of your fear and channel it into purposeful action. You can do this in two ways: by replacing negative thoughts with positive ones and by controlling your body posture.

Counter every negative thought with a positive thought. As fear mounts, you

Skydivers link up to make an aerial formation. Competitive formation skydiving is performed with teams of four, eight, or sixteen parachutists, who have to perform set routines in the air.

may discover an inner voice that encourages disaster, telling you, "You're going to die," or "You don't know what to do." The second these thoughts enter your head, counter them with positive statements—"I'm going to get through this," and "I can handle this." This will keep your mind focused and stop you from giving in to panic. The trick is never to let any negative thought go unchallenged and to counter a negative thought instantly with a positive one.

Help maintain control by taking charge of your posture. Stand up straight, or pull your shoulders back in a confident manner. Breathe deeply from your abdomen, and speak slowly and deliberately. Raise your head and focus your eyes sharply on the world around you. When you take action, move decisively and

THE STRESS RESPONSE

The human body has a very advanced system of responding to stress. When we encounter a frightening or threatening situation, the part of the brain known as the hypothalamus triggers the release of certain stress-response hormones into the bloodstream. These hormones flood the body and make it ready for life-saving action, which is often called the "fight or flight" reaction. The heart rate and breathing are increased to provide the body with more oxygen, which is necessary for strenuous action. Blood is diverted away from the brain and the skin (which is why frightened people turn pale), and is sent to the muscles, providing them with more physical energy. The liver releases the sugar glucose, a further source of energy. All these responses give a person tremendous energy and an increased ability to withstand pain.

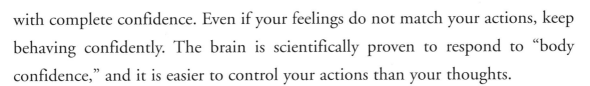

Knowledge is the best antidote for stress. Practicing for emergency situations will help when they are real.

with complete confidence. Even if your feelings do not match your actions, keep behaving confidently. The brain is scientifically proven to respond to "body confidence," and it is easier to control your actions than your thoughts.

By planning, visualization, and conquering your fear, you can put yourself in the right frame of mind for extreme sports. Leave nothing to chance, and refuse to let fear control you at crucial moments.

Physical Preparation to Prevent Injury

All extreme sports are tough on the body. Sprains, strains, dislocations, fractures, severe bruising, and lacerations are common injuries, but developing a strong, healthy body reduces the risk of these occurring.

There are three elements to preparing your body for extreme sports: flexibility, strength, and endurance. Flexibility and strength training make your muscles more resistant to damage, while endurance training helps you to resist injuries and accidents that result from exhaustion.

FLEXIBILITY AND WARMING UP

Flexibility training works by elongating muscles and giving them a greater range of movement. A flexible muscle is less likely to be damaged because it can undergo more strain before damage occurs.

Participants in extreme sports must work on flexibility to protect themselves from injury. For example, a climber requires excellent flexibility in the hips and shoulders to perform strenuous climbs without damage. A surfer or skier should develop good flexibility in the legs, particularly the **hamstrings** and **quadriceps**, in order to cope with the twisting forces exerted on the lower limbs when

Yoga is possibly the best program of flexibility training there is. It systematically stretches every muscle group in the body, while also promoting a calm and controlled state of mind.

changing direction. Even sports that seem at first to have no need for flexibility benefit from stretching exercises. Skateboarders, for example, will have fewer sprained ankles from falls if they work on their lower-leg flexibility.

Any stretching session should begin with a warm-up. Cold muscles are inflexible muscles and are more likely to rupture or be injured if put under sudden strain. A warm-up consists of two elements: light exercise to raise the temperature of the body, and stretching exercises to make muscles more flexible. Warm-up routines should be performed prior to undertaking any exercise. In extreme outdoor sports, these can be performed anywhere and take only about five minutes. If you are in a very cold climate, however, consider increasing your warm-up to around ten to fifteen minutes.

The first stage of the warm-up is to gently increase muscle temperature, heart rate, and breathing:

- Try jogging very gently on the spot for about five minutes. Slowly raise the knees higher as you go along, but do not let the thighs rise above a forty-five degree angle to the ground. Shake your arms loosely by your sides occasionally, to loosen up your shoulder and arm muscles.

Once your body feels warmer and your breathing is slightly heavier because of the effort, move on to some hip- and shoulder-loosening exercises:

- For the hips, stand with your feet shoulder-width apart, hands on your hips. Circle the hips in one direction as if you are spinning an imaginary Hula-Hoop, making circles that are as large as possible. Keep your shoulders as still as possible. Repeat ten times in one direction, then reverse and repeat ten times in the other direction.
- For the shoulders, make large circles forward with the arms, bringing the hands together in front of you and then brushing the hips at the bottom of the swing. Repeat in one direction ten times, then reverse.

This simple set of exercises will prepare your body for stretching. Different extreme sports demand different types of flexibility, but it is best to develop total body flexibility to protect yourself against injury. Attend flexibility training classes, such as yoga, to learn a full repertoire of stretching exercises. Then pick a simple set you can do anywhere, designed to stretch every major muscle group from your ankles to your neck.

Endurance is a key ingredient of all extreme sports. Distance running develops heart, lung, and muscle efficiency to cope with prolonged strenuous activity.

Ankles

For climbing, skateboarding, winter sports, and parachuting.

Sitting down, put the left ankle on top of the right knee. Hold the raised ankle with your left hand, and take hold of the toes and the ball of the foot with your right hand. Using your right hand, circle the foot around in one direction in large circles, repeating ten times. Then circle ten times in the opposite direction. Repeat for the other foot.

Hips

For climbing, surfing, skiing, and diving.

Stand upright with your legs in a wide "A" shape about two shoulder-widths apart. Bend forward from the waist and take your body weight on your hands.

To stretch the groin, push the knees downward slowly to the maximum stretch, hold for about ten seconds, then gently release the pressure and raise the knees.

Now slowly sink your hips downward, inching your legs wider and wider apart. Keep breathing deeply as you do this, and go down only as far as you can manage.

When you are at your limit, hold the position for five to ten seconds, and try to relax your muscles. You may find that you can go down a little farther after doing this. When you have reached your maximum stretch, come out of the stretch by walking your feet inward (maintaining your weight on your hands) until you are able to stand up.

Waist and back

For all extreme sports.

Stand upright, with your feet shoulder-width apart. Bend straight forward from the waist and lower your torso as far as it will go, keeping your back straight. Hold the legs and gently pull on them to go down farther. Hold the stretch for ten seconds, then move your body upright again. Next, place your hands against your lower back and stretch your body backward, looking up at the ceiling as you do so. Again, hold for ten seconds, then release.

Shoulder

For climbing, mountain biking, skiing, hang gliding, and parachuting.

Hold your left arm straight out in front of you, and hook your right forearm around the back of the left elbow. Keeping the left arm straight, use the right arm to pull it across your body until you feel a strong stretch in the shoulder joint. Hold for ten seconds, then release and switch arms.

CONDITIONING

In sports, "conditioning" is a term used to describe toughening up different parts of the body. For extreme sports enthusiasts, conditioning is a vital part of body preparation. What makes sports "extreme" are the massive demands placed upon muscles, bones, and the cardiovascular system. Conditioning exercises make these parts of the body powerful enough to meet the pressures they will face.

Resistance training is the primary tool of conditioning. This promotes the systematic development and strengthening of individual muscle groups used in a

Oblique crunches strengthen the sides of the abdominal muscles. Bring the elbow to the opposite knee, then repeat, switching sides with each repetition for as many times as you can.

Leg curls improve the strength of the thighs, hamstrings, and calf muscles. Begin totally flat with the ankles under the padded bar (left). Bring legs up slowly to a ninety-degree angle with the thighs (below), then release gently to the starting position.

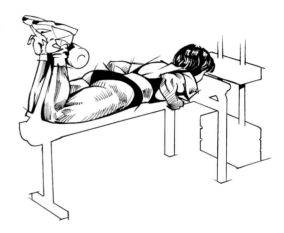

particular extreme sport. Basic resistance training involves exercises such as sit-ups, crunches, push-ups, and squat thrusts, using nothing but the body weight as the source of resistance. By contrast, weight training uses **free weights** or **weight machines** to develop the musculature. Weight training is generally better at isolating more individual muscle groups than are body-weight exercises, but requires proper equipment.

Weight training can be dangerous for the inexperienced or for people under the age of eighteen. We do not have the space here to look at every aspect of weight-training technique, but here are some important rules.

- Get expert training from a weight-training professional in a proper gym.
- Poor technique is the biggest cause of injuries in weight training. When you start a new exercise, practice it while lifting no weight at all until you can demonstrate proper technique.
- Do not attempt to lift very heavy weights. Instead, concentrate on lifting lighter weights with more repetitions.

- In any technique, add further weight in increments of 1–3 pounds (0.5–1.5 kg), and only after you can show at least eight repetitions using perfect technique and without undue struggle.
- Do not weight train more than three times a week, and keep training sessions under forty-five minutes.
- Breathe deeply throughout any lifting exercise. Breathe out as you push, pull, or lift the weight, and breathe in as you move the weight to its start position. Spend about three seconds on every stage—never lift weights with fast, jerky movements.
- Do a full warm-up before every weight-training session.

Barbell squats are used to improve leg strength. Keep the back as upright as possible throughout, and only use light weights.

Safety Equipment

Equipment in extreme sports may be all that separates you from serious injury or even death. All equipment should be selected under expert guidance and maintained in top working order.

Your first investment should be in safety equipment. Safety equipment falls into two categories: accident protection and environmental protection.

ACCIDENT PROTECTION

Equipment designed for accident protection is anything that protects the body from impact injuries or similar external damage. In this category, the most important piece of equipment is, obviously, a safety helmet.

Almost all extreme sports require a safety helmet. Even surfing—for which traditionally nothing more than swimming clothes are worn—is slowly accepting that head protection is advisable. Many serious injuries in surfing are caused when the surfer's head strikes rocks, other surfers, or other surfers' boards. These injuries would be easily prevented by wearing a light fiberglass or impact-plastic helmet, both of which are readily available. The same is true of skiing and snowboarding—a woolen hat provides no protection.

Have a helmet fitted in a professional sports store which understands your particular sport. Make sure it fits comfortably but securely. Adjust the straps to

The climber here wears full safety gear, including a climber's helmet and a climbing harness secured to a nylon rope. Climbing ropes can sustain tons of pressure before breaking.

make the helmet secure, check for any gaps in the fit, then shake your head vigorously. There should be no slippage or excessive movement when you do this. Helmets should have official safety certification stickers on them, such as the Snell standards or certification from the U.S. Consumer Product Safety Commission. These let you know that the helmets have been impact-tested and meet U.S. consumer standards.

Discard any helmet that has suffered a substantial impact. Even if the helmet looks all right, it may have minute hairline cracks, which will significantly reduce its strength if it is struck once again.

Sports such as skateboarding and rollerblading require additional protective equipment. Joints sustain hard blows from falls in these sports, so knee, wrist, and elbow pads are essential. The pads are usually fastened with Velcro. Regularly clean the Velcro of a

A cycling helmet properly fitted. Note how the straps are used to hold the sunglasses on to prevent them from being shaken off on rough ground.

Artic survival gear, including thermal bodysuit and head protector, and gloves secured to the jacket.

buildup of lint by brushing both sections with a stiff brush. If you do not do so, the pad will become looser and could come off during a fall.

Some extreme sports require more specialized protective equipment. Rock climbers, for example, usually have a bag of climbing chalk attached to their belts. The chalk helps to reduce sweating from the hands and can be a lifesaver. Whatever your choice of sport, get expert advice in advance about the appropriate protective equipment needed.

ENVIRONMENTAL PROTECTION

Extreme sports are usually performed outside, so the correct clothing for the climate is as important as any other piece of kit.

Cold climates

For the sub-zero environments commonly encountered in winter sports, always wear high-quality thermal clothing. Follow the layer principle of winter clothing: many thin layers of clothing trap heat better than fewer thick layers of clothing. Professional arctic explorers and mountaineers will wear about four layers, such as a thermal vest and underwear, a T-shirt, a woolen sweater, a thermal fleece, and waterproof clothing on the top.

No matter what winter sport you are involved in, always keep your head covered in a woolen hat (even beneath your safety helmet), and wear thermal gloves and socks at all times. About seventy percent of body heat is lost through the head, hands, and feet, and these areas are also prone to frostbite, so keep them warmly covered.

One important principle in cold climates is to wear "breathable" fabrics, such as Gore-Tex. These allow sweat to evaporate from the body into the atmosphere, but keep out rain and wind. Fabrics that do not breathe—particularly cotton—catch and hold sweat. When you exercise, they become soaked with sweat. Then, when you stop, the wet clothing cools and draws out heat from your body. Poor clothing therefore puts you at risk from hypothermia.

Pay special attention to your footwear. Proper winter boots should hold the ankle securely in a thick padded heel; be fully waterproof; and, ideally, should have tops made of fabric that breathes. Dual-density soles are useful if you are crossing rough ground because these cushion the legs against the impact of walking.

Take a good pair of sunglasses or snow goggles if you will be in snowy conditions. Sunlight reflecting off snow creates a blinding light and this can produce a condition known as "snow blindness": eyesight will become painful, your eyes will water, and your vision will be blurred. To stop this, all you need is a pair of dark lenses with adequate UV protection. For sports such as snowboarding and skiing, wear professional snow goggles—sunglasses may injure you if you fall.

Hot Climates

Hot climates present other challenges for participants in extreme sports. The main extreme sports conducted in hot climates are surfing and other aquatic

A lifejacket should be used in all aquatic extreme sports. Many lifejackets require maintenance every few years by a professional company to retain their buoyancy.

sports. The clothing for these sports is minimal—usually just bathing suits—but precautions must be taken against the power of the sun. Sunburn can seriously damage skin while intense heat may lead to **heatstroke**, a potentially fatal condition. Keep the body covered as much as possible to protect the skin. Wear a hat to keep the sun off your head. The hat should preferably have a wide brim or cloth extension at the back so that the neck is kept in shade. Exposing the head and neck to the sun for long periods is a principal cause of heatstroke.

Even if you are dark-skinned, apply regular sunscreen to prevent sunburn. Use a high factor sunscreen—number twenty-five or above; the factor number relates to the cream's protective strength. Make sure that you buy waterproof sunscreen so that it will not wash off in the ocean, and apply it at least every three hours.

Hot climates bring another peril—insect life. Biting and stinging insects are present in huge numbers in summertime or in tropical areas, particularly near the coast. While many of these are only a painful nuisance, some insects in tropical areas can carry disease. A drugstore will sell you insect repellent as a cream or spray. Apply it regularly, and especially toward night, when insect life tends to be at its busiest.

BUYING AND MAINTAINING EQUIPMENT

Extreme sports may require a huge investment in basic equipment. Some, such as bodyboarding, may need nothing other than a bodyboard costing just over $100. Other sports demand far more expensive purchases. A rock climber, for example, will have to buy climbing shoes, ropes, carabiners, pitons, a rock hammer, chalk bag, and protective clothing, as well as many other items, and will easily spend over a thousand dollars to be fully outfitted. While we do not have the space to look at the equipment needs for each individual extreme sport, there are some general rules to follow when buying equipment:

Inline skating requires the following safety equipment: professional safety helmet, elbow pads, and knee pads. These protect the areas most likely to be injured during falls.

- Before you purchase, try out different pieces of equipment within your club, so that you can find out what suits you. Take advice from experienced members of the club; they may help you to avoid mistakes when purchasing equipment.
- Be prepared to pay for quality.
- Buy equipment certified by a sport-governing body and a national safety organization. For example, rock climbing equipment should have a certification label from UIAA (*Union Internationale des Associations d'Alpinisme*).

This snowboarder has a high standard of protective clothing. The head and hands are protected against frostbite, while the snow goggles prevent particles of ice from entering the eyes at high speeds.

- Purchase only from reputable sporting outlets. If you do buy secondhand equipment, take an experienced member of your club with you to check the item over for any damage or problems.

Once you have bought your equipment, the equally important task is to maintain it. Maintenance means more than just keeping equipment clean; it means checking it regularly for damage, deterioration, and efficiency. Some equipment will need professional maintenance, but you should always check regularly for signs of wear and tear.

Learn maintenance techniques from an expert, and do not attempt any procedures unless you know exactly what you are doing. Remember, extreme sports are dangerous and your life may depend on your equipment. Take care of it.

ROPE CARE AND MAINTENANCE

Climbing ropes are a climber's lifeline. Made of nylon, they are incredibly strong and can withstand tons of weight. Yet they must be well-maintained if they are not to develop flaws with potentially lethal consequences:

- Never walk on a rope. The pressure of the foot scrapes the rope against the ground and can wear out rope fibers.
- Do not leave the rope in bright sunlight when not in use—the UV rays will weaken it.
- Check the rope regularly and frequently for any cuts or fraying
- Replace any rope after four years of very light use, or three months of extremely heavy use.
- Replace a rope immediately if it has already been used in a long fall.
- Wash a dirty rope with warm soapy water and allow to dry naturally.

Climbing equipment needs to be organized on a belt so that it is easily accessible during a climb. Always check each individual item for any signs of damage before the climb begins.

Common Injuries

Extreme sports expose the sportsman or woman to severe injuries and the possibility of being killed. Yet extreme sports also bring with them the risk of a wide range of minor injuries.

Impact injuries are the most common form of injury in most extreme sports. In snowboarding, for example, more than eighty percent of injuries result from falls or collisions with other objects or people. Parachutists run the risk of impact injuries to their lower limbs and backs when undergoing heavy landings.

More than many other sports, extreme sports pose the risk of **fractures** and **dislocations**, usually concentrated in the arms, wrists, legs, shoulders, and ankles. Fractures and dislocations usually have a clear set of symptoms:

- an excruciating, sickening pain in the affected area;
- heavy bruising and swelling;
- the injured person will be unable to move the affected limb;
- the limb or joint may be distorted or an irregular shape;
- bone may be sticking out of the skin.

Be careful when looking for such signs, however, as a fractured hand or foot may still be usable, and so go unnoticed. If severe pain continues in an injured area after an accident, arrange for an X-ray to see if any bones are broken.

Snowboarder Jeff Anderson, seen here with his arm in a cast from a snowboarding injury. Broken bones account for a very high percentage of injuries in extreme sports.

LEG FRACTURES

The lower leg has two main bones: the tibia and the fibula. The tibia is the larger of the two. A leg fracture may involve one or both of these bones.

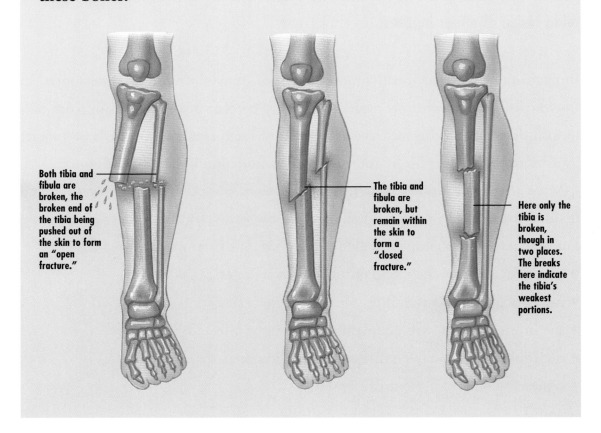

Both tibia and fibula are broken, the broken end of the tibia being pushed out of the skin to form an "open fracture."

The tibia and fibula are broken, but remain within the skin to form a "closed fracture."

Here only the tibia is broken, though in two places. The breaks here indicate the tibia's weakest portions.

Any break or dislocation requires professional treatment. Treatments vary according to the type of injury. For fractures, the doctor will first draw the broken bones back into their normal lines, perhaps using **traction** to do so, and then apply a plaster or fiberglass cast around the injured limb to keep it immobilized while it heals. In more serious fractures involving shattered bones, surgery may be used. Fragments of bone are relocated and pinned into place with surgical screws and/or metal plates, which are attached directly through or onto the bone itself.

Your doctor will tell you when the cast, brace, or frame will be removed—usually after a period of a few weeks—and when you can gently resume physical training. Initially, you should avoid the activity that caused the injury in the first place. The muscles, **ligaments**, and bones will have weakened during your period of inactivity, so heavy exercise is liable to result in further injury. Do light weight training and flexibility exercises first to restore the limb's strength and range of motion (**R.O.M.**). Steadily increase the pressure on the injured limb over a period of several weeks until there is no pain during exercise.

For dislocations, the doctor must also relocate the joint into its normal position, then immobilize it. The healing period for dislocation varies according to the amount of damage done to ligaments and muscles, but after an immobilization of four to six weeks, the athlete can usually begin light exercise and any recommended physical therapy.

Younger athletes are more vulnerable to repeated dislocations because ligaments may have been weakened or stretched. About eighty-five percent of athletes aged sixteen to twenty-five who suffer one dislocation go on to suffer another dislocation in the same place at a later date. If damage is extensive, the recovery period will extend to several months. Sometimes surgery may be required to prevent further injury.

As with fractures, dislocations require gradual recovery. Do not overload the joint until strengthening and flexibility exercises have brought it up to par. If using weights to strengthen the joint, start off with weights well within your comfort range and add further weights in increments of 1–3 pounds (0.5–1.5 kg). Your aim is not to test whether you have healed, but purely to build up the range of movement and stability in the limb before doing heavy exercise.

ELBOW JOINT

The elbow joint flexes the lower arm with a hinge-like movement.

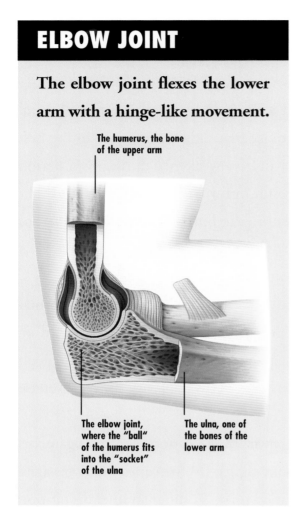

The humerus, the bone of the upper arm

The elbow joint, where the "ball" of the humerus fits into the "socket" of the ulna

The ulna, one of the bones of the lower arm

OVERUSE INJURIES

An extreme sports enthusiast runs the risk of a whole series of overuse injuries. Overuse injuries occur when a muscle, ligament, **tendon**, bone, or joint is put under repeated strain until it suffers damage. These injuries tend to occur gradually, often with minor symptoms that are easily ignored at first. As a rule, treat any pain or discomfort seriously if it is persistent. The range of overuse symptoms includes:

- weakness, stiffness, pain, or limited movement in a joint or limb;
- shooting or burning pains in a particular muscle group;
- pains accompanied by nausea or headaches;
- clicking or popping noises during movement in a joint, usually accompanied by pain, while the joint itself feels unstable;
- a sensation of something physical prohibiting movement in a joint;
- numbness in a joint such as the wrist or ankle.

Each extreme sport tends to have its own set of overuse injuries. Rock climbing, for example, causes injuries mostly in the fingers, hands, arms, and shoulders.

The fingers are among the most commonly injured parts of climbers. The ligaments holding the finger joints together can be ruptured from undergoing prolonged stress and weight-bearing.

Muscles and tendons in these areas are repeatedly put under great strain during climbs. The fingers are vulnerable to ruptured tendons, the result of holding too much weight. The elbows can become unstable because the climber's climbing style builds the **biceps** more than the **triceps** (or vice versa), resulting in an imbalance that weakens the joint.

In skiing, the knees are most at risk, accounting for around twenty-three percent of all skiing injuries. The knees not only endure hundreds of tiny impacts during each ski descent as the skis bump over the snow, but may be twisted through falls or sudden changes of direction as well.

For overuse injuries, and sudden injuries to muscles or ligaments such as sprains and strains, the athlete may often be able to use a standard method of self-treatment. Remember to follow your doctor's advice to the letter, and take the following directions as a general guide only.

1. Rest, Ice, Compression, Elevation (R.I.C.E.)—up to two weeks

- As soon as the injury becomes a problem, stop the activity immediately and rest the injured joint or limb completely.
- Apply ice packs to the injured part for no more than twenty minutes at a time, three or four times a day.
- Wrap a **compression bandage** around the injury and take **anti-inflammatory** medication such as ibruprofen.
- Raise an injured limb on a high surface (such as a chair). All these measures will reduce swelling and aid recovery.

2. R.O.M exercises—from three days to six weeks

Gently work the injured joint or muscle through its full range of movement. In the case of an ankle, for example, practice turning your foot in circles, and pulling it backward and forward. Try more complex movements as well, such as writing the alphabet in the air with your big toe. The goal is to increase pain-free flexibility to normal levels.

Wrapping a compression bandage around a sprained ankle and elevating the injury helps to reduce swelling and encourages healing.

3. Resistance exercises—from one to six weeks

Having increased the flexibility of an injured body part, increase its strength using steady weight training. Go very slowly. Begin with only rubber-band resistance exercises or the lightest of weights, and progress onto moderate weights only as the body allows. Do not attempt any extreme weight-lifting activities.

4. Return to training—from one to six weeks

Return to your sport, but attempt only light sessions to test whether the injury has healed properly. Slowly increase the level of training over a period of several weeks until you feel that everything is back to normal.

Although this four-stage process may take a long time—up to five months, in fact—do not rush it. Injuring the same part of your body several times will usually result in a permanent injury or even disability, and could force you to stop your sport altogether.

ENVIRONMENTAL INJURIES

Many extreme sports take their challenge from confronting wild or dangerous elements of the natural world. In mountaineering, snowboarding, and skiing, as well as many aquatic sports, the biggest threat is **hypothermia**. This is a drop in the body's core temperature and is usually caused by exposure to extreme environmental cold.

If the temperature at the body's core—in other words, the vital organs in the torso—is forced below the healthy range, normally 96.8°–100.4°F (36°–38°C) by freezing temperatures, rains, snows, or immersion in cold water, the body can seriously malfunction.

In any climbing injury, the biggest danger is often from the elements. Keep the injured person warm and in a secure place until professional rescue personnel arrive on the scene.

The first signs of mild hypothermia will be in your behavior. You become tired and listless. Strange mood swings may take hold—one minute happy, almost elated, the next depressed or aggressive. You will find it hard to concentrate and focus on tasks, and your arms and legs will become uncoordinated and clumsy. You will be pale, and your skin very cold to the touch.

At this stage, you can stop the progression of hypothermia before the condition becomes too serious. First and most importantly, you must get out of the cold, wind, and rain. If you have a tent, put it up and get inside. If not, find shelter. If sitting on the ground, place a piece of material or other barrier between yourself and the earth. Change any wet clothing for dry. Wrap yourself in a blanket (or any other warm material) to prevent further heat loss, and snuggle up close to your companions so that you can share body heat. Sit near a fire if one is available, and have warm drinks and food. These measures should restore your normal body temperature, at which point you should head for home.

SEVERE HYPOTHERMIA

Severe hypothermia has a much scarier set of symptoms, and only other people will be able to help you. You will become incoherent and incapable of rational thought. Your color will be deathly pale. You will stop shivering because your body has run out of energy. Finally, you may lapse into unconsciousness, and death will not be far away. If you are the one providing first aid, you must get professional medical treatment immediately. Do not try to move the person unless it is absolutely necessary, and contact the emergency services. Meanwhile, wrap the person in warm, dry clothing or, ideally, a sleeping bag. Your aim is gently to warm him or her, so move them close to a heat source. Place any warm materials or storage containers—such as hot-water bottles, thermal packs, or even warm stones (heated over a fire and then wrapped in thick cloth)—against places where blood flow is close to the surface of the skin. These places include the wrists, armpits, groin, back of the neck, small of the back, and between the thighs. Keep the casualty in a rested position, as warm as possible until help arrives.

DEHYDRATION

Of course, extreme heat can be just as dangerous as extreme cold. The biggest danger is dehydration, a very serious condition. If our fluid intake is less than our output, the body starts to malfunction. If left unchecked, dehydration can lead to the failure of major body organs and death. Early danger signs are: a raging thirst; a pale and sweaty complexion; a low urine output (the urine will also be dark in color); nausea and headaches; and a sense of fatigue and confusion.

As soon as you sense any of these symptoms, get out of the sun and into the shade. Rehydration is simply a matter of drinking enough water. Sip the water—do not gulp it, as your dehydrated stomach may reject the sudden intake of water and so vomit it back up, making your dehydration worse.

Keep your clothes on, even if soaked with sweat; they will help reduce water loss through sweating. Try not to talk too much and keep your mouth closed, as a lot of body water is lost in microscopic droplets of water when we breathe out.

Do not underestimate how much you will need to drink. For a full day's physical activity in a hot climate, you will need at least 10–12 pints (5–6 l) of water to keep from being dehydrated. You will know when you have drunk enough because you will urinate frequently and the urine will be a light color.

Take a comprehensive first-aid course if you are going to participate in any extreme sports. Knowing what to do in an emergency could save your life and the lives of your companions.

WOUNDS AND INFECTIONS

Extreme sports enthusiasts commonly receive injuries that bleed. For relatively minor wounds, first stop the bleeding, and then take action to prevent infection:

- **STOP THE BLEEDING**

Press down on the wound with a clean pad of material, preferably a sterilized medical dressing. Maintain this pressure until the bleeding has stopped. Elevate the wounded area above the level of the heart. This reduces blood flow to the injury and helps to stop the bleeding.

- **PREVENT INFECTION**

First wash your hands with soap and water, or clean them with an antiseptic wipe. If the wound is small, wash it under running water and pat it dry. Clean the area around the wound with soap and water, and try not to touch the wound with your fingers. (Do not use water on any wound that has been bleeding heavily; it will only encourage further bleeding.)

Try not to breathe or cough over the wound. If there are minor pieces of dirt in the wound, try to pick them out with sterile tweezers or wash them out with water. Do not try to remove any deeply embedded objects—these will need the attention of a doctor. Cover the wound with adhesive tape or a sterile bandage.

Careers in Extreme Sports

Making a living from extreme sports is more precarious than trying to do it in any other sport. For a young enthusiast, the main ways to bring in serious money are through winning competitions and getting sponsorship.

There are several reasons why extreme sports rarely offer financial security. The first is that many of them have few participants when compared with "normal" sports. Extreme sports can be expensive to fund, and sports such as mountain climbing and parachuting may require thousands of dollars of expenditure to maintain. Furthermore, the danger element of extreme sports is not suitable for everyone, so only a few dedicated individuals try them. For both of these reasons, the numbers of extreme sports enthusiasts tends to be low, which means that there is less money going into the sport and less money to give out in sponsorship and competition prizes.

However, there are exceptions. Skiing, surfing, and skateboarding are huge international sports. Of all the extreme sports, skiing is the most mainstream: it is part of the Winter Olympics and offers world-class skiers the chance to make a living by winning competitions. So if your chosen sport is less mainstream or has fewer participants, what are the best ways of making it your profession?

Racing against the clock, slalom racer Heidi Zeller-Baehler of Switzerland cuts close to a slalom post during the prestigious Women's World Cup Alpine Championships.

SPONSORSHIP

In extreme sports, sponsorship is perhaps the most important method of making money. Sponsorship is when a business, organization, or individual provides funds or other help for the activity of an individual or group. Sports sponsorship is not just for the big names. Every year, thousands of small or unusual sporting events are sponsored by companies and organizations on a local or regional level. Sponsors are more likely to do this if the event benefits a charity. Extreme sports are a great way of raising public awareness of different charities, and many companies enjoy helping charitable causes.

How do you acquire sponsorship? Here are some general pointers. First, write down a list of companies and individuals who might be willing to sponsor your event. Look in the *Yellow Pages* and business directories (available through local libraries), or make a note of any businesses sponsoring other events. Draw up a list and approach each company in turn. First, telephone the company and ask the receptionist the name and address of the person who deals with sponsorship. Contact that person in writing initially, and explain exactly what it is you want to do; what you want—if it is money, specify how much and indicate how it will be spent; and what is in it for them. If you do not hear back in about a week, telephone the person and ask for a response.

Getting sponsorship is a difficult business. Companies may receive hundreds of requests each year for sponsorship, and they are cautious about the people to whom they give money. Here are some ways to increase your chances:

- Keep your initial letter to no more than one page. Businesspeople are often very pressed for time, and they will not want to read a long letter.
- Do not feel you have to ask for money. Ask instead for equipment, free advice, or simply discounts on products.

TONY HAWK

Tony Hawk has become the world's most famous name in skateboarding. He started around the age of nine and pushed himself extremely hard to learn more and more advanced moves. A supportive father made traveling to competitions much easier for Tony. His father was so supportive that he also founded two skateboard associations—the California Amateur Skateboard League and the National Skateboard Association.

Tony's ability on, and dedication to, the skateboard was superb. He had turned professional by the time he was fourteen. Tony has won more than 100 professional skateboarding competitions, has his own skateboarding equipment companies, and brings in six-figure sponsorship. He is also featured in the video game *Tony Hawk Pro Skater*.

Tony Hawk performs a typically spectacular aerial maneuver on the half pipe.

- Emphasize why sponsorship might be good for the company. Companies want publicity, so contact lots of radio and television companies and ask them to agree to cover your activity. Tell the sponsorship company about this—they will be interested in getting their company name into the media.

- Ask a local or national celebrity to do some publicity for your event. Again, the increased media coverage will make the company more willing to help you.

- Be persistent. Keep working through your list of companies, even if you receive lots of rejections, and be prepared to build up your relationship with a particular businessperson slowly.

If you are fortunate enough to receive sponsorship, make sure a responsible adult administers the money for you. Spend any money exactly as you promised you would—otherwise, the sponsoring company may take legal action against you.

Always take legal advice through the guidance of your parents or school if you have to sign a contract. A contract can affect the way you do your sport for years to come, so it must be checked line by line.

COMPETITIONS

There are two final methods of earning your living through extreme sports: competitions and coaching. Every extreme sport—even "extreme ironing"—has international competitions and sometimes significant levels of prize money. In surfing, the Rip Curl Pro competition held in Australia has a prize that typically totals $500,000. Some FAI parachuting games have over $22,000 of prize money. In skiing, the prizes can go into the millions.

Earning money from such competitions basically means either winning or placing as a close runner-up. This is a difficult task in any sport and requires a huge amount of dedication. Most competitions are conducted under the rules of

Competitive white-water canoeing involves negotiating twenty to twenty-five "gates" — markers suspended over the water — along the length of a watercourse in the fastest possible time.

at least one national or international organization. Make sure that you find out which organization is running each competition. The rules of competition will vary according to each governing body, so learn exactly what is expected of you before you arrive at the competition. Other than that, you will need to train exceptionally hard to give yourself a winning chance.

Winning competitions is rarely the reason why most people do extreme sports. Some people make a living, and a very good one, from their sport, but most do extreme sports to relax and free their minds from the everyday. Like all sports, do not compete if competing will keep you from enjoying yourself.

Glossary

Anti-inflammatory: Medications are described as "anti-inflammatory" if they reduce swelling in an injury.

Barbell: A long metal bar on which weights are attached for weight training. It is picked up with a two-handed grip.

Belaying: A climbing technique in which a climber is attached to a rope securely fastened to a pin or other point above.

Biceps: Large muscles on the inside of the upper arm which flex the arm and forearm.

Carabiners: A spring-loaded metal link, through which climbers secure ropes.

Compression bandage: A bandage that holds a swollen joint or muscle tightly to reduce the swelling.

Descender: A climbing device used to control the speed of a climber's descent down a rope.

Dislocation: An injury in which a joint in the body is wrenched or knocked out of its normal position.

Fracture: A break or split in a bone.

Free-fall: In parachuting, free-fall refers to a long drop during which the parachute is not opened.

Free weights: Weight-training equipment consisting simply of a bar onto which weights are placed.

Hamstrings: The group of three muscles set at the back of the thigh.

Paragliding: A sport in which people use a wing-like parachute to make a flying descent from an airplane or a high place.

Heatstroke: A dangerous increase in the body's core temperature, taking it well above its healthy range of 96.8°–100.4°F (36°–38°C).

Hypothermia: A dangerous drop in the body's core temperature, taking it below its healthy range of 96.8°–100.4°F (36°–38°C).

Ligament: A short band of tough body tissue, which connects bones or holds joints together.

Pitons: A metal spike knocked into rock to support a climber or rope.

Quadriceps: A large four-part muscle on the front of the thigh, which is used to extend the leg.

Rappelling: A method of descending a rock face by walking down the face while attached to a long double rope that is securely fastened to a point above.

Rip tide: A powerful water current formed where two or more currents meet.

R.O.M.: Abbreviation for range of motion, describing exercises designed to restore full flexibility to a damaged joint or muscle.

Sky surfing: An extreme parachute sport using a board very similar to a surfboard that is attached to the feet and used for steering through the air during a free-fall drop.

Snowboarding: A winter sport that uses a single wide board to "surf" across the snow.

Tendon: A cord of body tissue connecting a muscle to a bone.

Traction: In medical practice, traction involves pulling gently on a broken or dislocated limb to draw it back into its natural alignment.

Triceps: The muscles on the back of the upper arm.

UV rays: Ultraviolet rays, a type of damaging radiation in sunlight.

Weight machines: Machines providing various resistance exercises, used in weight training.

Further Information

USEFUL WEB SITES

The folowing web sites offer numerous articles and advice on extreme sports events, equipment, and news:

www.adventuretime.com

www.awezome.com

www.extreme.com

www.extremesports.com

The Web sites listed on this page were active at the time of publication. The publisher is not responsible for Web sites that have changed their address or discontinued operation since the date of publication. The publisher will review and update the Web sites upon each reprint.

FURTHER READING

Carlson, Keith et al. *Extreme!: The Ultimate Guide to Action Sports.* Chicago: Triumph Books, 2003.

Faigenbaum, Avery and Wayne Westcott. *Strength and Power Training for Young Athletes.* Champaign, Illinois: Human Kinetics, 2000.

Gutman, Bill. *Being Extreme: Thrills and Dangers in the World of High-Risk Sport.* New York: Citadel Press, 2002.

Levy, Allan M. and Mark L. Fuerst. *Sports Injury Handbook: Professional Advice for Amateur Athletes.* New York: John Wiley & Sons, 1993.

Tomlinson, Joe. *The Ultimate Encyclopedia of Extreme Sports.* London: Carlton Books, 1996.

THE AUTHOR

Dr. Chris McNab is a writer and editor specializing in sports, survival, and other human-performance topics. He has written more than twenty-five books, and recent publications include *Survival First Aid, Martial Arts for People with Disabilities, Living Off the Land*, and *How to Pass the SAS Selection Course*. Chris lives in South Wales, U.K.

THE CONSULTANTS

Susan Saliba, Ph.D., is a senior associate athletic trainer and a clinical instructor at the University of Virginia in Charlottesville, Virginia. A certified athletic trainer and licensed physical therapist, Dr. Saliba provides sports medicine care, including prevention, treatment, and rehabilitation for the varsity athletes at the University. Dr. Saliba holds dual appointments as an Assistant Professor in the Curry School of Education and the Department of Orthopaedic Surgery. She is a member of the National Athletic Trainers' Association's Educational Executive Committee and its Clinical Education Committee.

Eric Small, M.D., a Harvard-trained sports medicine physician, is a nationally recognized expert in the field of sports injuries, nutritional supplements, and weight management programs. He is author of *Kids & Sports* (2002) and is Assistant Clinical Professor of Pediatrics, Orthopedics, and Rehabilitation Medicine at Mount Sinai School of Medicine in New York. He is also Director of the Sports Medicine Center for Young Athletes at Blythedale Children's Hospital in Valhalla, New York. Dr. Small has served on the American Academy of Pediatrics Committee on Sports Medicine for the past six years, where he develops national policy regarding children's medical issues and sports.

Index